# BRIXHAM

## *of Yesteryear*

### Chips Barber

GW00392505

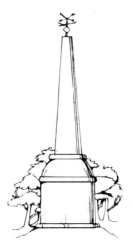

OBELISK PUBLICATIONS

## OTHER TITLES IN THIS SERIES

## OTHER TITLES ABOUT THIS AREA

***For a current list please send an SAE to***
***Obelisk Publications, 2 Church Hill, Pinhoe, Exeter EX4 9ER***

### Plate Acknowledgements:

All pictures belong to Dave K. James, apart from pages 19 (bottom), 23 (top), 27 (top) and 30 (top), which have been kindly supplied by Frank Potter.

*Dave James would like this book to be dedicated to his darling wife, Marian.*

*First published in 1995, reprinted in 1999 and 2006 by*
*Obelisk Publications, 2 Church Hill, Pinhoe, Exeter, Devon*
*Designed by Chips and Sally Barber*
*Typeset by Sally Barber*
*Printed in Great Britain*
*by Avocet Press, Cullompton, Devon*

# BRIXHAM

## *of Yesteryear*

Brixham is the sort of place that gets into the blood of its residents. Having collaborated with Brixham Museum and History Society on *A Brixham Album*, I also know how much enjoyment people got from that book, so felt that there was room for a further publication along the same lines.

There are many people who collect old picture postcards of their town, and Brixham-born Dave James is such a person. He has amassed an impressive collection, which spans a century of memories, of people and places, of faces and features. In this book we include a sequence of pictures from his archive to illustrate what the port was like in a "Brixham of Yesteryear". We have tried to avoid a repetition of pictures even though some views are bound to be similar. However, this little book should prove to be equally popular for anyone who has an interest in Brixham, as there are many unusual views of things that have long since gone. We hope that you will enjoy this trip, not only down Memory Lane, but all around Brixham's narrow, quaint streets, over its steep hills and around its spectacular shoreline.

Let's start with this picture, looking down from the heights of Parkham Hill towards the harbour. Note the scene of sails rising high above the distant breakwater!

How times change! Here we have four pictures featuring Higher Brixham from those days when the pace of life was decidedly slower than it is today. Above we have Summer Lane, about 1905, looking like a place that's miles out into the countryside, not a thoroughfare on the fringe of a town that seems to be ever-growing upwards and outwards.

Below is a view of Milton Street, with the road's surface looking very muddy – not that many wayfarers are appearing to use it.

The view above is the one seen looking from Windmill Hill towards Higher Brixham, where the church can be spotted on the right side of the picture. The windmill was built about 1797, one of a number in the district that utilised the reliable prevailing westerly wind. When it was a working windmill it changed hands several times. We know that Barnabus Tuckerman Green owned it in 1835 along with the adjacent Little Rey field. It is believed that the cap and sails of this windmill were blown off during a storm in 1870.

The card was sent in October 1907; since then many of the green spaces that existed are now covered in housing. The one thing that hasn't changed is the number of steep hills in and around Brixham!

The sender of the card below posted it at 2.00 p.m. on 18 December 1905 to an address in Torquay, phones not being in common usage then. It simply bore these glad tidings: "Nellie, a girl this morning (noon) 5 minutes to 12, Will." The view is of Annie Tolcher's Cottage, named after a lady noted for her poetry.

Above we are still in Higher Brixham, which is instantly recognisable for not a lot has changed since this 1905 postcard view. The drinking fountain has gone and a telephone box has replaced it as a concession to modern living. The junction also sees a lot more traffic these days!

Below is New Road looking down the hill towards Brixham town. The card is a visual reminder that this thoroughfare was once blessed with considerably more trees than it has today. A cyclist is seen casually riding, in a relaxed fashion, up the centre of a much narrower road.

Here we have two more views of New Road, but both much closer to Bolton Cross. The postcard above was posted in September 1906 to the sender's father in Guernsey. The message relates that his loving daughter, Lilian, has placed a notice in the local newspaper advertising for a servant. The view is looking on the main road out of Brixham, whereas the one below looks the other way. A posse of children, possibly in their Sunday best, have gathered together in the road for this picture.

Many people will have fond memories of those days when it was possible to come all the way to Brixham by steam train. The one that plied up and down the branch line from Churston to Brixham was "The Whippet".

Above, a steam train, engine no. 1470, later to be scrapped, is seen leaving the main line at Churston to start the short journey along the branch line into Brixham. The last steam train to travel along this branch did so without much ceremony, on 11 March 1961, before being replaced by a diesel unit.

Below is a view of Churston Village, taken early in the twentieth century. At the end of the road is a bridge, which carried the Brixham branch line.

Here we have two pictures of Brixham Station, one with a steam train, engine no. 1452 and the other a diesel, the type that served the line until its closure in 1963. The last train carried more than a hundred passengers and was given a rousing send-off. Children waved flags and noisy fog detonators were exploded to create a memorable occasion. Having seen Brixham's parking and traffic problems in more recent years, had it been kept open, the line may well have been a real godsend. However, it's always easy to be wise after the event…

In its heyday the railway brought thousands of visitors to the town. Brixham, as a resort, always has had a lot to offer, with its grand scenery. On this page we have two views of the St Mary's Holiday Camp, taken just after the Second World War. The top picture shows some 'compact' chalets, each of them appearing to be semi-detached! Fortunately the views are a lot more spacious: this one looks across the cliffs to Sharkham Point.

Below, holidaymakers are enjoying a 'wheelbarrow race' on the weekly sports day held at the camp. It all looks like hard work, with the participants having to cope not only with an upward slope, but also with being on the side of the hill.

The Dolphin Holiday Camp is closer still to Sharkham Point. Its tennis courts feature in both of these views, again taken not long after the war. Both also show neat regimented lines of uniform chalets from a time when people who had survived the rigours of the war years were beginning to come out to enjoy life again.

The message on the back of the above card was full of praise for the standard of the camp and of the people working there. The only note of dissent was that everybody seemed to be so much better at tennis than the sender of the card!

With the next quartet of pictures we return not only to the town centre, but also to an earlier era. On this page we have two views of Fore Street, the one above looking towards the harbour, the one below towards Bolton Cross. It is possible to make many observations about the changes that have occurred in Fore Street, but it is noticeable, in the picture above, that there were a lot more houses in 1905 in this main shopping street. The sender ignored the traditional type of message to comment on the thinness of the girls in the foreground of the picture. She suggested that they required 'a little filling out'.

The top picture is of the harbour end of Fore Street; although taken many years ago, there is something reassuring to note that, even then, you could snap away quite merrily at the colourful spectacle of the harbour and then pop into the shop on the right of this view to have the film developed and printed.

Below is another favourite subject for those who like to take pictures of quaint buildings. Ye Olde Coffin House has served many uses throughout the years, and is a unique building, if the claim on the notice-board on it is to be believed, for it says "Ye Olde Coffin House only one in England."

The next sequence of photographs all feature the harbour area, a place that was certainly the hub of Brixham life. The picture above shows the fleet of red-sailed Brixham fishing smacks in port. The old fish market can be seen stretching a considerable way along the quayside, with the number of people there indicating a fish auction is in progress.

The picture below is an altogether different scene, with the buildings in neat, straight terraces dominating the picture.

Here we have two familiar views of Brixham, the angle favoured by a great number of photographers when set the task of producing the standard "Brixham picture". In the top one, vehicles help to date the scene, parked where vehicles dare not park today. William of Orange is protected by his railings and a couple of cannons.

The bottom card was posted in Plymouth in late August 1931, but it is probable that the picture was taken a lot earlier, perhaps on a special occasion as one of the houses towards the right, at the top, is flying a large flag.

Brixham has always been synonymous with fishing, and these scenes capture that fishy flavour. Above, an auction of wooden kits of skate is taking place early in the morning at the fish market. The fish have probably been caught from the nearby fishing grounds of Start Bay, or from Salcombe Ground.

Below, would-be purchasers of the skate look long and hard at the fish while considering what sort of prices might be realised.

In the past it was almost impossible to see across the inner harbour when the smacks filled it almost to capacity. A veritable forest of ships' masts and riggings existed.

Above are the fishermen preparing to go to sea, a dangerous occupation at the best of times. Brixham once had more orphans, per hundred head of population, than any other place in the country.

But it wasn't always hard work, for below we have a group of fishermen pictured near the fish market, possibly after the auctions have finished. Between them they sport a variety of headwear, but most wear the customary fishermen's jerseys. The shed at the end of the fish market was used for storing nets and other fishing equipment.

A wide range of allied activities took place in and around the port, in addition to the fishing: sail-making, rope making, shipbuilding and repairing, and some more unusual activities. The chimney, as seen in both these pictures, belonged to the ice factory, an important commodity for keeping fish fresh.

The bottom postcard was sent in July 1910, the sender having had a wonderful time. She wrote of the sixty or so fishing smacks that she saw in the harbour "with all shades of brown sails – they were most wonderfully picturesque."

The top picture is a variation on the same theme as the ones on the opposite page, but taken from a different angle.

The bottom picture shows the *Duke of Devonshire* in Brixham Harbour in August 1936. She was one of a pair of paddle steamers, the other being the *Duchess of Devonshire*, that was made by the firm of R & H Green of Blackwall, London. There had been a growth in the number of visitors coming to the coast, the railways having played their part in making the journeys generally more speedy and more comfortable. This influx meant that it became quite the fashion to go on rides along the coast. The *Duke* (built 1896) and the *Duchess* (built 1891) graced the waters off the coast of Devon, the *Duchess* being a more familiar sight on the eastern seaboard of Devon. The *Duke* was based at Torquay and covered the western side, with Brixham, Salcombe and Plymouth being favourite ports of call.

The top picture is an over-the-rooftops view of the Inner Harbour. The area of Furzeham is full of buildings peering over each other to catch a glimpse of the sea. Freshwater Quarry, now a car park, is a working quarry in this postcard view, which was sent in September 1917. It was posted to Ramsgate in Kent, and the correspondent noted that there were three Ramsgate smacks in the harbour at the time of her day trip to Brixham. "Jack" sent the view below, showing himself to be the master of brevity for all he wrote, apart from an address in Southsea and the date, 23 August 1928, was "Some place!" From that we don't know what he thought of Brixham as it's somewhat ambiguous.

The two pictures on this page make this sort of book so worthwhile in that it is highly unlikely such a scene as this will ever be repeated. These graceful fishing smacks make the Outer Harbour look so purposeful. The top picture shows more of the land as it reaches out to its conclusion in the sheer limestone bastion-like cliffs of Berry Head. Although there are buildings along Berry Head Road, and the occasional one higher up, the scene has changed considerably since then.

Once again we have two similar views, the top one being much older as the postcard was sent during the First World War. Just to the right of the centre of this view can be seen Prospect Road rising up from Overgang after one of the steepest zig-zag bends in Devon.

The bottom one shows that Brixham has grown, but even this 1950s card is well out of date with so many changes having since occurred in the foreground.

*Brixham of Yesteryear*

Here we have a scene of celebration as yet another Brixham-built vessel awaits its launching. Brixham had three main shipyards in the early part of the twentieth century, which gave employment to about 150 workers. The trawler above is one that was built at Upham's and is the *We'll Try*. It was owned by W. R. Brokenshire who was at No 1, The Quay at that time – now it's No 5!

The original caption on the postcard view below simply says "Bay View Camp. Brixham". The fields, where the camp lies, only show a small number of tents. Today it is a very different place: just one of a number of Pontins' camps in the area. The lifeboat station can be spied to the bottom left of the picture.

It's time to play "Spot the Difference" for these two pictures taken from Round Top, although both old, are taken some years apart. The top one isn't dated, but the bottom one carries a postmark for August 1921, although the picture was taken some time earlier. The Breakwater was extended to its present length and completed in 1916. The person who sent it posted it in the Netherlands to another address in that same country. It is amazing to think that it has come home to Brixham after all these years! Like the one at the top of the opposite page, it shows us a scene where the Breakwater is only partly finished, this construction reaching a length of some 3,000 feet in 1916.

*Brixham of Yesteryear*

Here a paddle steamer collects or drops off passengers at the Breakwater Beach. It was possible, using both the *Duke* and the *Duchess of Devonshire*, to cover most of the South Devon Coast in a day's sailing, provided that the conditions remained fair for the cruise and that you worked your schedule out carefully to make the transfer from one vessel to the other. Sometimes walking the extremely flexible, bouncing gang plank from the paddle steamer to the beach was an adventure, and it was not unknown for some passengers to finish up in the briny!

The building below, "Miss Hayman's Tea House", was a popular retreat for refreshments. It was situated very close to the Berry Head House Hotel; this scene shows it as it was in August 1908. A group of people are sat at tables in the grounds blissfully unaware that in later years the house would be demolished to become a car park.

Here we have two more pictures of the popular Breakwater Beach. The one above looks along the beach towards the Breakwater with a small row of beach huts storing all the essentials for a day's relaxation at this sun trap.

Below is a very similar picture to one that appeared on Page 38 of *A Brixham Album*, but a comparison shows that this is many years later, the facilities having been extended and improved.

Shoalstone's bathing pool, farther along Berry Head Road, has had its ups and downs over the years. The top picture shows it as a very basic structure indeed, but that hasn't stopped a number of people from taking advantage of safer-than-the-sea waters.

The bottom picture show a new, pristine pool, complete with candy-striped beach huts and deck chairs. In the lower centre of the picture a person seems to have plenty of spare capacity in the striped robe they are wearing, possibly following a swim.

It's a bit of a climb from Shoalstone to the heights of Berry Head, but it is worth the effort for this Country Park, created in 1970, has much to make a visit worthwhile. The lighthouse, which first shone its radiant beam in early May 1906, was nicknamed "Captain Hoare's Baby" because this good man did much to get a warning light placed here. Although it is a very small lighthouse, it stands on limestone cliffs about 200 feet high, so its range is still considerable – 40 miles some say.

Below, and opposite top, is the fine Fort Café where many people for many decades have enjoyed refreshments. It must be about the most solid café in the kingdom, as it was built as a guardhouse for this cliff-top fort. For more details of the history of Berry Head and its buildings you should read my book *Brixham*, part of a trilogy that covers the three towns of Torbay. This card, posted in August 1921, also shows the well-worn path that leads to the lighthouse and former coastguard station.

The people are well kitted out for the weather, which suggests that this picture was taken on one of those days of summer when the weather was not warm or fine enough to cast off outer layers, but just about suitable enough to sit out for a quick snack, alfresco fashion, to pose for a photo.

The picture below is from the other side of Brixham and is taken at Fishcombe Cove, the numbers on this small beach showing it to be a sheltered spot. It is hard to imagine that shipbuilding once took place in this small cove, just as it did at nearby Churston Cove.

All Saints Church started life as a chapel-of-ease in 1816. However, its status changed and it was consecrated as a parish church in 1824. The first incumbent, its most famous, was the Revd Henry Francis Lyte who wrote several hymns including, "Abide With Me". The tower of the church, a most obvious landmark, was added in 1906, the same year as the lighthouse was established on Berry Head.

The Town Hall at Bolton Cross was built in 1887 for £3,000 and has given the town good value in a number of uses. Here, the traffic outside is of a very different nature to that which queues back at the traffic lights there these days.

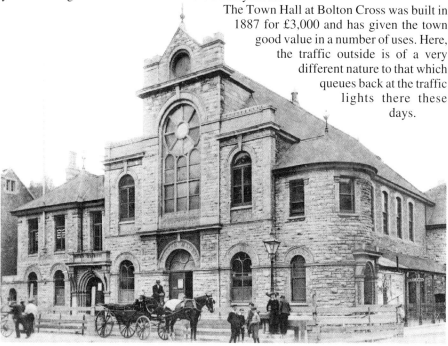

Top left is a view of Higher Street from almost a century ago, a scene that has changed largely because of a block of flats that have been built here since. The postcard of the "New Quay Inn" was posted in July 1924. Today it's the Hole in the Wall. Below is a multi-view card, typically showing a variety of scenes from a bygone Brixham.

And so we come to the end of this particular look back at Brixham's past through its old pictures, with these two postcards that will mean something special to many Brixhamites. Both cards can be read quite easily, so there is little need to explain what they are about. The Flanders' poppies that decorate the stone were donated by the British Legion from Pinhoe, in Exeter. The name Brixham is known all over the world for its fisherfolk have travelled the oceans and spread its name. But most have come home, as there's no place like it! If you have enjoyed this little jaunt down 'Memory Lane', don't forget to look out for Parts II and III!

ALL SAINTS CHURCH,
BRIXHAM,
BUILT TO THE MEMORY OF
REV. H.F. LYTE.

BERRYHEAD HOUSE,
BRIXHAM,
WHERE
ABIDE WITH ME
WAS WRITTEN

H old thou Thy Cross, before my closing eyes;
Speak through the gloom, and point me to the skies;
Heaven's morning breaks, and earth's vain shadows flee;
In life, in death, Oh Lord, abide with me."

THE ORIGINAL OF THE LAST VERSE OF THE HYMN
"ABIDE WITH ME."
NOTE THE WORD "SPEAK".

BY REV. H. F. LYTE